BEYOND THE BEACH: THE WIT AND WISDOM OF NEVIL SHUTE

Bill Levy

Graham Thorley's portrait of Nevil Shute Norway
(Permission by the owner, Dan Telfair)

This book is dedicated to the memory
of
my parents,
Esther and Leonard R. Levy

TABLE OF CONTENTS

FOREWORD

Bill Levy has written a very interesting book about my Dad, Nevil Shute, ***Beyond the Beach: The 'Wit and Wisdom of Nevil Shute'*** designed as an introduction to his works. After a brief biography which takes up about one third of the book, he gives a one sentence review of the plot of the book under discussion, then short excerpts from it designed to give the flavour of that book, and this he does very well. It is an interesting concept well designed to give prospective new readers, and those returning after a considerable absence the motivation to read, or re-read these stories.

I would highly recommend this book to anyone who is curious about the 'Prince of Storytellers' of the mid twentieth century.

I am privileged to be asked to write the foreword to this exciting new book.

Heather Mayfield
December 2011

PREFACE

Over the past fifty years, Nevil Shute's novels have provided me with a sanctuary from many of the absurdities of contemporary life, given me much of my moral base, and helped to expand my personal horizons. But I never encountered another "Shutist" until 1999.

In January of that year, I attended the Nevil Shute Centennial in Albuquerque, New Mexico and moderated the program, "Introducing Nevil Shute to 21st Century Readers." Dan Telfair, the Centennial's coordinator, described that gathering, organized to celebrating the centennial of Nevil Shute's birth, aptly:

> We were not a gathering of adults come to honor our favorite author. We were a lot of children who had always been forced to play alone at home with our favorite toys, now brought to a program full of other children with the same sort of toys, all wanting to play the same sort of games. We

were beside ourselves with
the joy of it all.

I left the Centennial with a desire to do something to help "spread the word" about Nevil Shute and decided to write this book. Now, thirteen years later, having overcome publication difficulties and obtained permissions, I am finally able to share my passion for Nevil Shute and, hopefully, stimulate others to explore and re-explore his world.

To this end, I am donating ten percent of any profits I make from this book to The Nevil Shute Norway Foundation's libraries towards the purchase of Nevil Shute's books, films, and audiotapes. The Foundation is an organization of Shutists dedicated to increasing an awareness and appreciation of Mr. Shute. The website is www.nevilshute.org.

INTRODUCTION

British novelist Nevil Shute (1899-1960) is remembered primarily for his novel *On the Beach*. But he wrote over twenty other fascinating novels that are still extremely relevant today.

Beyond the Beach: The Wit and Wisdom of Nevil Shute is divided into two sections. The first section, "Beyond the Beach," is an overview of Nevil Shute's life and career and consists of (1) a biographical sketch of Nevil Shute including a brief analysis of his work, and (2) a discussion of reasons why he should be read today and tomorrow. The second section, "The Wit and Wisdom of Nevil Shute," is divided up into nineteen sub-sections. Each sub-section contains quotations from one of Shute's books. These sub-sections are organized chronologically and begin with a short synopsis of the novel.

This book contains 115 quotations that demonstrate Nevil Shute's perceptions of people, places, and ideas; they also illustrate his subtle humor, his gentle yet masculine use of language, his unique sense of timing, and his genius for succinctly capturing a universal concept with deceptive simplicity.

I have elected to utilize these quotations from nineteen of Nevil Shute's works of fiction beginning with his first mature book *Ruined City*/American title: *Kindling* (1938). It is my hope that experiencing these portions of Shute's works will stimulate an interest in reading and rereading some of the most entertaining, addictive, touching, and pertinent fiction of the twentieth century.

The Nevil Shute books whose quotations are used in this volume are listed below with their British titles first, then the American titles, and the date of publication.

Ruined City/Kindling (1938); *What Happened to the Corbetts/Ordeal* (1939); *An Old Captivity* (1940); *Landfall* (1940); *Pied Piper* (1942); *Pastoral* (1944); *Most Secret* (1945); *Vinland the Good* (1945); *The Chequer Board* (1946); *No Highway* (1948); *A Town Like Alice/The Legacy* (1950); *Round the Bend* (1951); *The Far Country* (1952); *In the Wet* (1953); *Requiem for a Wren/The Breaking Wave* (1955); *Beyond the Black Stump* (1956); *On the Beach* (1957); *The Rainbow and the Rose* (1958); *Trustee from the Toolroom* (1960)

Nevil Shute was born Nevil Shute Norway but in this book I refer to him as Nevil Shute.

BEYOND THE BEACH

Nevil Shute was the most popular British writer in the world during the 1940s and 1950s. According to his obituary in *The New York Times*, "no other English writer of his day approached the combined sales of the novels he turned out year after year." Perhaps because of that popularity, his fiction has been often underestimated. Shute's sober masculine imagery, his neurosis-free protagonists, his gentle humor, and the lack of angst in his balanced narratives appear dated at first but this is deceptive. The messages, themes, characters, and perspectives of Nevil Shute's novels are relevant and significant today, over 50 years after his death.

Shute had the unique capacity to combine an astute and pragmatic knowledge of technology with an optimistic humanism and, quite often, with a compelling sense of mysticism. His books continually emphasize the power of the individual to shape history while his genuine and generous protagonists provide excellent heroic prototypes. Nevil Shute had an uncanny ability to predict the future. He also had the skill to sculpt stories that open up his readers' minds.

Any discussion of Nevil Shute's work must begin with his own life. As Julian Smith stated in his Twayne Series volume on Shute, "Though none of his novels is explicitly autobiographical, all of his books come directly out of his life, his work, his times, his environment, and his interests in a way that is seldom observable in other writers."

"Nevil Shute: His Life and Works"

Nevil Shute was born Nevil Shute Norway on January 17, 1899 in Ealing, a suburb of London. He did not come from a traditional literary background, but several members of his upper-middle class family were writers. Shute's father, a senior civil servant in the postal service, wrote several travel books, a critique of *The Divine Comedy*, and a history of the postal-package service. Shute's mother wrote a volume describing the family's experiences during the Sinn Fein rebellion in Dublin in 1916, and his grandmother wrote children's books.

Shute stuttered from the age of five or six and, according to his autobiography, encountered intolerable experiences from his peers and unsympathetic masters. His daughter, Heather Mayfield, has maintained that the stuttering plagued him all his life. In 1912, his family moved to Dublin when Nevil's father became head of the postal service in Ireland. Shute attended the prestigious Shrewsbury School from 1913 to 1916. In 1915, his only sibling Fred, three years older than Nevil, died in France during World War I.

In 1917, Shute trained at the Royal Military Academy as a Royal Flying Corps gunnery officer, but eventually failed his medical exam because of his stutter. In August 1918, he enlisted in the infantry, but the war ended before he was sent to France.

After the war, he attended Balliol College at Oxford from 1919 to 1922 and took third class honors in engineering. In 1923, he joined the de Havilland Aircraft Company as a junior stress and performance calculator.

Shute worked on details of aircraft design at de Havilland for eighteen months and then moved on to Vickers Ltd. Here he was involved with the design of the R.100 airship (dirigible) and was responsible for translating theoretical calculations into engineering practices. He soon moved up into management and remained with Vickers until 1930. Vickers was a private company in direct competition with the British government in airship development. (The government's airship the R.101 crashed in 1930 while Vickers' R.100 successfully flew to Canada and back without any serious problems). Shute was deeply affected by these experiences and devoted a great deal of attention in his autobiography to the R.100-R.101 controversy:

I was thirty-one years old at the time of the R.101 disaster, and my first close contact with senior civil servants and politicians at work was in the field of airships, where I watched them produce disaster. That experience still colours much of my thinking. I am very willing to recognize the good in many of these two classes, but a politician or a civil servant is still to me an arrogant fool till he is proved otherwise.

During the 1920s, Shute devoted his free time to flying and to writing four adventure novels about aviation. *Stephen Morris* and *Pilotage* were rejected repeatedly in the 1920s; they were later published together posthumously as *Stephen Morris* in 1961. *Marazan* (1926) and *So Distained*/American title: *The Mysterious Aviator* (1928) were the first two of Shute's novels to be published. Both the engineer and the novelist shared the same goal of improving the country's aviation standing.

In 1930, he left Vickers and founded the aviation company Airspeed Ltd. In 1931, he married physician Frances Heaton and published *Lonely Road*, the last of his early adventure-espionage novels. Shute's two daughters, Heather and Shirley, were born in 1932 and 1935. In 1934, he was elected Fellow of the Royal Aeronautic Society for his pioneering work on retractable landing gear.

In 1936, *Lonely Road* was filmed in Britain as *Scotland Yard Commands* starring Clive Brook. As a result, Shute returned to writing after a hiatus of five years. He wrote *Ruined City*/American title: *Kindling* (1938), in many ways Shute's first mature book. Its hero, Henry Warren, is a banker-philanthropist who is willing to go to prison in order to aid others. He is the first of Nevil Shute's intensely altruistic protagonists. And as Shute scholar Julian Smith observed, Warren is, like Shute himself, "a slightly disoriented pioneer in the age of monopoly."

1938 was a pivotal year for Nevil Shute. He had been involved in considerable friction with other members of Airspeed's Board of Directors, and, according to his autobiography, "began to lose interest in the company I had brought into being." He resigned from the company in early 1938 and received a substantial settlement. His views of his experiences in the aviation industry are revealing:

> I have never gone back to manufacturing and I shall probably not do so now, for that is a young man's game. Industry, which is the life of ordinary people who employ their civil servants and pay their politicians, is a game played to a hard core of rules; I am glad that I had twenty years of it as a young man, and I am equally glad that I have not had to spend my life in it till I was old. My gladness is tempered with regret, for once a man has spent his time in messing about with aeroplanes, he can never forget their heartaches and their joys, nor is he likely to find another occupation that will satisfy him so well, even writing novels.

Ruined City was Shute's first commercial success, and an American film studio bought the movie rights in 1938. Although the picture was never made, Shute suddenly had the financial flexibility to write full time. In his autobiography, Nevil Shute matter-of-factly relates:

> Now several thousand pounds had dropped into my bank account for doing what to me had been a relaxation from real work....For ten years, if I chose, I could just sit in the sun drinking Pernod, and not bother about work. It seemed incredible, but it was all quite true.

In 1939, months before the outbreak of World War II, Shute published *What Happened to the Corbetts*/American title: *Ordeal*. This book vividly describes (and correctly prophesied) the devastating effect of air raids upon an English city and an English family, and it soon became a best seller. Also in 1939, Shute began working as a volunteer developing experimental weaponry with Sir Dennistoun Burney.

In 1940, Shute published *An Old Captivity* and *Landfall*. The former tells the story of an early transatlantic airplane flight and expedition following the odysseys of the ancient Viking explorers. It is the first of Shute's novels with an extensive out-of-body experience. (Shute's daughter, Heather Mayfield, has maintained that her mother, Frances, influenced him in developing these "paranormal" situations in his books: "As an engineer, he was very grounded. She was not so much.")

Landfall utilizes Shute's expertise with fighter and bomber tactics and naval weapons to give the storyline substance. *Landfall* was later filmed in England in 1948.

In 1940, Shute volunteered for the Royal Navy Volunteer Reserve hoping to be placed in a minesweeper. However, once his engineering background was discovered, he was assigned to the Department of Miscellaneous Weapon Development, where he directed the engineering department for the next four years. Colleagues of Shute remember him as an extremely strong, capable, and imaginative administrator with a wry and witty sense of humor. During World War II, he and his section were responsible for researching, designing, and adapting numerous significant weapons and devices. His obituary in *The New York Times* stated, "Among his successful devices were a remote-control target for gunnery practice, a multiple rocket for use against dive bombers, and a rocket spear for use against submarines."

While he worked on these secret weapons, Shute wrote three more World War II novels: *Pied Piper* (1942), *Pastoral (*1944), and *Most Secret*, written in 1942 but due to security restrictions, not published until 1945. The first two books became major wartime best sellers in England and the United States.

Pied Piper describes the adventures of a seventy-year-old Englishman who rescues seven children of diverse nationalities and backgrounds from the Nazis in France at the time of Dunkirk and brings them safely to England. The book was filmed in 1942, and veteran character actor Monty Woolley received an Academy Award nomination for his work in the title role. This book and the movie markedly expanded Nevil Shute's popularity throughout the English-speaking world. *Pied Piper* was later refilmed in 1990 as the television movie *Crossing to Freedom* starring Peter O'Toole.

The equally popular *Pastoral* pictures the war of an RAF pilot who divides his time between rest and romance in the English countryside and violent air battles over enemy-held Europe.

Most Secret depicts the background of several undercover missions to France and, according to Shute, was written as pure propaganda. Shute later maintained that

Most Secret was from the technical point of view, "the best formed book I ever wrote." The book's protagonist Charles Simon is the typical Shutian hero: realistic, competent, taciturn, and altruistic.

Most Secret was very significant for Nevil Shute. Due to the wartime censorship, the novel was not published for three years. This angered Shute and he was eventually transferred to the Ministry of Information in 1944 after he vocalized his frustrations.

In June 1944, Shute went to Normandy to observe the invasion as a correspondent for the Ministry of Information and wrote several articles describing D-Day and its aftermath. In 1945 he wrote *Vinland the Good*, a retelling of the Norse sagas of *An Old Captivity*. He wrote this story in the form of a filmscript. Also in 1945, Shute traveled to Burma to write propaganda articles for the Ministry of Information. Shute utilized his Burmese experiences in *The Chequer Board* published in 1946.

The Chequer Board's protagonist John "Jackie" Turner is an English businessman with a criminal background who has been told by his doctors that he has less than a year to live. Turner decides to search for three old wartime acquaintances to see if they need his help. This book is Shute's first novel with significant non-European characters and settings, and indicates a more mature and compassionate view of the world beyond England.

During the next five years, Nevil Shute wrote three important novels: *No Highway*, *A Town Like Alice*/American title: *The Legacy*, and *Round the Bend*.

In 1947, Shute spent several months touring the United States. From September 1948 through March 1949 he flew his own plane across Europe, Asia, and Australia, accompanied by the writer James Riddell who later wrote a detailed account of this trip in his book, *Flight of Fancy*. Shute used these travel experiences to stimulate ideas for future plots, settings, and characters, but he was also searching for something else: a new place to live. He was unhappy with England and its socialism and high income tax, and desired a change. In 1950, Nevil Shute moved permanently to Australia with his wife and daughters.

In 1948, Shute published an aeronautical engineering suspense thriller, *No Highway*. This book relates the story of an unlikely hero, an eccentric aeronautical researcher, who questions the safety of a new transatlantic airliner. Shute's knowledge and passion for this topic is apparent and helps to explain his astonishing ability to make a book about theoretical research addictive reading. *No Highway* was filmed as *No Highway in the Sky* in 1951 and starred Jimmy Stewart, Glynis Johns, and Marlene Dietrich. The book eerily and accurately predicted the Comet aviation disasters of the 1950s.

A Town Like Alice (1950) is Shute's most famous book after *On the Beach*. This novel tells the story of a young Englishwoman, Jean Paget, her World War II experiences in Malaya, and her later life in Australia. Both Jean and the other main character, Australian Joe Harman, exhibit the five senses of the Shute protagonist: common sense, a sense of integrity, a sense of courage, a sense of resolve, and a sense of humor. It was filmed in 1956 in England with Virginia McKenna and Peter Finch and in 1980 in Australia for television with Helen Morse and Bryan Brown.

In 1951, Nevil Shute published *Round the Bend*, which is considered by many Shute readers to be his most significant work. This book focuses on a messianic ground engineer who spreads his spiritual teachings of careful maintenance all over Asia. *Round the Bend* not only shows how open-minded Shute had become on race and religion; it reveals his need to question many accepted European views and values, and to address complex spiritual and moral quandaries.

In the 1950s, Shute's life and work revolved around Australia which represented to him the hopeful future, while England depicted the tired past. These perspectives were reflected in his novels *The Far Country* (1952), *In the Wet* (1953), *Requiem for a Wren*/American title: *The Breaking Wave* (1955), and *The Rainbow and the Rose* (1958).

The Far Country is a romance that contains a condemnation of living conditions in England after World War II and is a tribute to the optimism of Australia and her new immigrants. It was filmed in 1986 starring Michael York and Sigrid Thornton, thirty-four years after its initial publication.

In the Wet continues and broadens Shute's pro-Australian themes, but is more significant due to its mysticism, its uncompromising call for a superior quality of politics and politicians, and its uncanny glimpses of the future.

Requiem for a Wren is Shute's dark, gloomy final farewell to World War II; he once remarked that this novel is the same story as *A Town Like Alice* with a tragic ending. (His short novel, *The Seafarers*, written in 1946/1947 and published in 2002, is an earlier attempt to depict the post-war lives of the young veterans of World War II).

The Rainbow and the Rose is Shute's valediction to the aviation of his youth and the last of his novels in which he utilizes the technique of a protagonist experiencing dream-like trances, allowing this character to intimately experience another person's past thoughts and actions.

In 1954, Shute wrote the first of a proposed two-volume autobiography titled *Slide Rule: The Autobiography of an Engineer* describing his life to 1938. Shute always considered himself an engineer who wrote; one of his early statements in the book was, "Most of my adult life, perhaps, all the worthwhile part of it, has been spent messing around with aeroplanes." Although this autobiography focuses on his engineering experiences, it shows much about Shute the writer. Among the titles he considered for his life's story were *Slide Rule into Typewriter, Not All Fiction, A Calculator Looks Back, The True Success,* and *Travelling Hopefully.*

In 1954, Shute traveled in western Australia exploring the oil fields and then journeyed through the American Rockies in anticipation of writing a novel about an American geologist's romance with an Australian girl. This book, *Beyond the*

Black Stump (1956), reveals a repudiation of the American Dream and also demonstrates Shute's questioning of values he had long accepted and advocated. According to Shute scholar Julian Smith, this novel shows that the engineer and the novelist both "realize for the first time that the technology he had espoused all his life might not be capable of creating an earthly paradise."

Nevil Shute's most famous work, *On the Beach* (1957), contemplates the ultimate abuse of science and technology. This book describes the last living survivors of World War III awaiting nuclear fallout in Australia. The book was a major best seller and, together with the 1959 film starring Gregory Peck, Ava Gardner, and Fred Astaire, broadened Shute's audience, introducing millions of new readers to Nevil Shute's understated sanity. The film was remade as a television drama in 2000 starring Armand Assante, Rachel Ward, and Bryan Brown.

Shute had a heart attack in December 1953, another one in November 1955, and a stroke in December 1958. Nevil Shute Norway died in Australia of a cerebral hemorrhage on January 12, 1960 while working on the third chapter of his twenty-fourth novel, *Incident at Eucla*. According to his notes, this novel would have used a Second Coming to help Australia thwart nuclear destruction. It appears Shute was too much of an optimist to allow mankind to destroy itself after all.

After his death, Shute's final work, *Trustee from the Toolroom* (1960), was published. The critic of *The Atlantic* described it as "a story remarkable for its lucidity and amiability." The book tells the tale of Keith Stewart, another unassuming Shutian everyman, who travels across the world to fulfill a family responsibility. Unaware of his strengths, this very uncomplicated, competent, and stable protagonist is the embodiment of the Shute hero.

"Why Shute Should Be Read"

There are several reasons why Shute should be read today and tomorrow.

(1) Nevil Shute had the rare ability to combine the engineer's expertise in the technical world with the novelist's universe of imagination, drama, and romance. *The Encyclopedia Britannica* observed he "showed a special talent for weaving his technical knowledge of engineering into the texture of his fiction narrative." The critic C. P. Snow found Shute to be a bridge between two cultures - an engineer who could speak to the general reader as well as to professionals.

In a 1960 essay on Shute in *The John O'Louden's Weekly*, Phyllis Bottome critiqued Shute's literary career:

> No one in modern literature is quite like him. Nevil Shute was in the first place a stunt writer; that is to say, an author who writes from personal skill of a technical craft; and who writes with such an intensity of

understanding that he infects his readers with a degree of interest scarcely less than his own... But Nevil Shute had far greater literary qualities to back his documentary knowledge than most stunt writers. He had an imaginative choice of very unusual subjects, and the selective power of the true artist in fitting all his characters into appropriate incidents. His novels are beautifully constructed and his characters convincing.... What made Shute a major novelist was that he had acquired this double faculty. Technical knowledge was a passion with him, but imagination was the bread of his life.

Nevil Shute used his technical background as a foundation to create his artistic vision. He approached writing as an objective engineer, but as he created a story, he added restrained emotion. He combined his astute and pragmatic knowledge of technology with an optimistic humanism and, quite often, with a compelling sense of mysticism.

Shute's characters are not just pilots, scientists and engineers who are comfortable working and living with machines and machinery; they are individuals who address the difficult dilemmas about technology, and especially the crucial question, "Can science and humanity co-exist?"

(2) Nevil Shute's books continually emphasize the power of the individual to shape history. In *Vinland the Good*, Shute discloses his philosophy of history in the words of an iconoclastic teacher:

> People in history were not a different race from you and me. Your history books deal mostly with the great people, the Kings and Princes and the Ministers of State. They're just the froth upon the surface; the Kings and Princes and the Ministers - they don't mean much. History is made by plain and simple people like ourselves, doing the best we can with each job as it comes along. Leif went out to get timber to build cowhouses, and found

America.   That's how real
people make real history.

Shute's protagonists do their jobs, affect
other people, and often make history: the
young pilots of his early books aid the
growth of the fledgling aviation industry and
several help thwart dangerous international
plots; in *Ruined City/Kindling* one banker
rescues an entire city from financial ruin; in
Vinland the Good outlaws and slaves
discover America; in *No Highway* an
eccentric scientist saves thousands of lives;
in *Round the Bend* one ground mechanic
starts an international airline and another
changes the lives of countless believers; and
in *A Town Like Alice/The Legacy* a former
typist builds a town in the isolated
Australian Outback.

(3) Nevil Shute bestowed upon his readers
unforgettable moral protagonists who
provide excellent heroic examples for
today's world.   Most of Shute's major
characters devote their time, their skills,
their money, and their lives to help others.
They have great personal integrity, humility,
and a strong empathy for others. They have
good common sense and use rational
thought to combat challenges and solve
problems.   They make difficult decisions
and great sacrifices, and put others' welfare

before their own. They are memorable human beings whose generosity and compassion show us the true meaning of heroism.

(4) Nevil Shute had an uncanny ability to predict the future. In several of his novels, his vision of the future is astounding. In *What Happened to the Corbetts/Ordeal*, he tells the story of an English family enduring murderous bombing raids, raids that England actually experienced a year after the book was published. In *No Highway* he describes an airliner crash due to structural fatigue. Four years later, four de Havilland Comet airliners crashed. It was later discovered that the cause was structural fatigue. In *In the Wet* published in 1953, he writes about 1982 when the British are discontent and antagonistic toward their monarchy. This book contains astonishingly accurate descriptions of Queen Elizabeth, Prince Philip, and Prince Charles. And in Shute's most famous work of prophecy *On the Beach* (1959), although his prediction that World War III lasted for thirty-seven days in 1962 was incorrect, that was the year of the Cuban Missile Crisis.

Shute had a purpose behind these prophecies. In his "Author's Note," at the end of *In the Wet,* he wrote, "No man can see into the future, but unless somebody makes a guess from time to time, and publishes it to stimulate discussion it seems to me that we are drifting in the dark, not knowing where we want to go or how to get there."

(5) Shute scholar Julian Smith maintained that Shute's one great message "was that of the need for understanding, for a posture of openness to the possibilities of life. In his best novels, he demanded that his readers accept the outer limits of the human mind's potential...."

Reading Shute's works chronologically, one perceives within Nevil Shute a growth away from a closed perspective characterized by racial, social, religious, and cultural biases, and a movement toward an open attitude. In many of his post- World War II novels, Nevil Shute battles racial and cultural prejudices as he introduces his white Anglo-American readers to characters of color who are responsible, thoughtful, and, like all of Shute's significant creations, both sensible and sensitive human beings.

Nevil Shute also acquainted his readers with numerous unusual psychic phenomena such as the significance of dreams, extrasensory perception, the transference of personality, and reincarnation. His uses of the transference of souls in *An Old Captivity, In the Wet*, and *The Rainbow and the Rose*, the Ouija board in *No Highway*, and the religious imagery in many of his novels but especially in *Round the Bend*, provide his readers with the opportunity to have their own out-of-body experiences.

Nevil Shute widened his readers' perspectives, broadened their viewpoints, and forced them to reconsider prejudicial stereotypes. Shute's protagonists are open to change, open to progress, open to the East, open to the unknown, open to the future. Throughout his life, the two Nevil Shutes, the engineer and the writer, always remained faithful to the first credo of every good engineer: keep an open mind.

(6) Finally, most of Shute's books are an ode to optimism. It is the positive hard-working person who succeeds, the cynical complainer who fails. Although several of his books do not have particularly happy endings, his protagonists never remain stagnant and are usually rewarded for their dreams, vision, and ability to change.

Nevil Shute's hopefulness and his belief in people can be seen in all of his books. Nowhere is this more apparent than in the closing paragraph to his war novel *Landfall*:

> So let them pass, small people of no great significance, caught up and

swept together like dead leaves in the great whirlwind of the war. Wars come, and all the world is shattered by their blast. But through it all young people meet and marry; life goes on, though temples rock and the tall buildings start and crumble in the dust of their destruction.

THE WIT AND WISDOM OF NEVIL SHUTE

Ruined City/ Kindling (1938)

In order to save the economy of a floundering northern British city during the Depression, a renowned banker involves himself in a shady financial scheme that may ruin his reputation and send him to prison.

THE NEED FOR WORK
"There's only one cure for starvation—work! If only we could get some work back here! That's the only thing that allows us to be human and foolish, as you've got to be."

Chapter Four

SEWER RATS
"I've never been to the Balkans. Are the people nice out there?"

He shrugged his shoulders. "A man like me, going on business, never meets the real people. If I had to judge the Visgrad people by the ones I've met I'd say they were a lot of sewer rats." Chapter Eight

ONE GETS TO A STAGE

"One gets to a stage, later on in life, when the things one used to work for don't quite fit. I've got all the money I could ever want to use.... One can't just give up working. And so one's got to find a motive, an excuse for going on doing the job one knows.... There's only one thing really worth working for in the City. That's to create jobs."

Chapter Ten

THE THING MOST WORTH DOING

"I believe that that's the thing most worth doing in this modern world," he said quietly. "To create jobs that men can work at, and be proud of, and make money by their work. There's no dignity, no decency or health today for men that haven't got a job. All other things depend on work to-day: without work men are utterly undone."

Chapter Ten

HOME

It lies in the nature of a man to make himself a home.   Chapter Thirteen

What Happened to the Corbetts/Ordeal (1939)

A young English couple and their three children experience the horrors of modern warfare and urban bombing in this eerie and accurate prophecy of World War II events written before the war began.

NEW IDEAS FOR A NEW KIND OF WAR
A new war … brings new conditions and the old ideas won't fit. Then you've got to hack out a new set of ideas for yourself, and do the best you can. Put away the red coat, and invent a khaki one.   Chapter Three

A DOCTOR DURING WARTIME
"I'm working sixteen hours a day where I'm most needed, at work I can do damn well. I never worked better in my life. I don't get any money for it. I don't expect anyone will even remember that I've done it. This is what I came into the world for. Whatever I do after this will be – just spinning out my time."   Chapter Three

LIFTING ONE'S SPIRITS
It takes a very little thing to lift the spirits of a man. He was leaving his home for an

indefinite time, leaving his house, his business, and his office ruined and abandoned, flying with his family from death by high explosive or disease, journeying towards a future all unknown. And yet, his heart was light. Routine was broken; there would be no more drafting of conveyances for a time, anyway. The sun was shining after the rain of the night. He had a hundred pounds in his pocket. And, above all, he was going to his boat.

Chapter Four

WARS ARE WON

"Wars are won by men walking on their flat feet, with a rifle and a bayonet...."

Chapter Four

A SORT OF IMPRESSION

"I don't know if in passing through the world you leave a mark behind you. A sort of impression. I'd like to think so, because I think we must have left a good one. We're not famous people and we've not done much. Nobody knows anything about us. But we've been so happy. We've lived quietly and decently and done our job. We've had kids too – and they're good ones."

Chapter Eight

An Old Captivity (1940)

A young aviator, a professor, and his daughter explore Greenland in the 1920s in search of artifacts of the Norsemen explorers. Their expedition combines adventure, romance, and an extensive out-of-body experience for the pilot.

DREAMS
Dreams are useful, if you don't try to read too much in them…. Many of us have strange experiences once or twice in our lives, and we don't call ourselves abnormal.

Chapter One

SUCCESS IN LONG-DISTANCE FLYING
For the first time Alix began to understand long-distance flying. It was not courage, or resourcefulness, or ability that counted in this game, though they were necessary subsidiary qualities. It was the capacity to work efficiently at tiring, menial tasks upon the ground that makes great flights success.

Chapter Four

GREAT FLIGHTS
Great flights were made by men who kept their heads.   Chapter Five

WORK

The work came first. He had a job to do.... it would take every ounce of energy that he had in him. He knew that very well by now. Everything else must be subordinate to that. Chapter Seven

A DIFFICULT UNDERTAKING

Each step of the journey, considered at the time, did not seem very difficult or very arduous; it was only when you came to look back upon it as a whole that you saw what a job it had been. Chapter Ten

DRINKING IN BEDROOMS

[In Canada], You aren't allowed to drink it [a bottle of liquor] in a public place, or with your meals in the restaurant. So when you want to have a drink, you throw a party in a bedroom. It's the normal thing to do ... It's a vicious law, this one that makes you drink in bedrooms. It puts ideas into one's head.

Chapter Ten

Landfall (1940)

In England during the early years of World War II, the flirtatious relationship between a pilot and a barmaid develops into a complicated romance involving class differences, military secrets, and naval disasters.

RIGID DISCIPLINE

It was quite true what Enid said; he didn't understand the young. A great part of his life had been spent in dealing with them, moulding them into the old naval form in the old naval way. He was too good a technician not to realize that methods must change with the years. ... He had continued blindly on the old, worn tracks of rigid discipline because he lacked the understanding to thrash out a method of his own for dealing with young officers.

Chapter Seven

PLEASURE FROM THE SEA

In their lives they had taken pleasure from the sea; that it now wrapped them close could not be altogether ill.

Chapter Ten

THE PERSERVERENCE OF EVERYMAN

So let them pass, small people of no great significance, caught up and swept together like dead leaves in the great whirlwind of the war. Wars come, and all the world is shattered by their blast. But through it all young people meet and marry; life goes on, though temples rock and the tall buildings start and crumble in the dust of their destruction. Final Chapter

Pied Piper (1942)

An elderly but feisty Englishman caught in France at the time of the German invasion in 1939 saves numerous children, strangers to him, from the Nazis.

PLEASURE IN CONVERSATION
"When you are tired there is a pleasure in conversation taken in sips, like old brandy."

Chapter One

A CHILD'S WHISTLE
It was clear that in their [the children's] minds a whistle was the panacea for all ills, the cure for all disease of the spirit.

Chapter Four

THE ENGLISH
"So really, monsieur, none of these little ones have anything to do with you at all?"

"I suppose not," he said, "if you like to look at it that way."

She pressed the point. "But you could have left the two in Dijon for their parents to fetch from Geneva? You would have been able then, yourself, to have reached England in good time."

He smiled slowly. "I suppose so."

She stared at him. "We French will never understand the English," she said softly.

Chapter Seven

BEAUTY

"You can call a sunset by a filthy name, but you do not spoil its beauty."

Chapter Ten

THE ENGLAND HE KNEW

"But they're in such a *state*! Have you seen their poor little heads? My dear, they're *lousy*, every one of them." There was a shocked pause. "That horrible old man—I wonder how he came to be in charge of them."

The old man closed his eyes, smiling a little. This was the England that he knew and understood. This was peace.

Chapter Eleven

Pastoral (1944)

An RAF pilot during early World War II lives a dual life flying dangerous bombing missions over Europe and romancing and fishing in the quiet English countryside.

PIKE AND ROACH

Spinning for pike was more in keeping with the quick energy of the pilot; moreover you could eat stuffed pike. It was true that Phillips ate the roach, but it was generally conceded that roach were an acquired taste. If you happened to like eating cotton wool stuffed with mud, you liked eating roach. Chapter One

LOVE

Everybody at Hartley aerodome was deeply interested in Love except perhaps the Adjutant and Flight Officer Stevens, and one or two others more than twenty-five years old. For the majority of the Wing, Love was as essential a commodity as petrol, and much more interesting. Chapter Four

THE SUREST SHIELD

The surest shield that any bomber pilot could possess was peace of mind.

Chapter Five

A MAN OF FIFTY

A man of fifty is seldom a match for a young girl.　　　　　Chapter Five

TEAMWORK

A good polo team is best made up of friends.　　　　　Chapter Six

THE VERY STUFF OF ENGLAND

I ... moved up the room to see what he was looking at. All I saw was a little service truck, and the young pilot who had come out of the room before me standing by it, talking eagerly to a W. A. A. F. section officer in the sunlight. There was nothing else but that.

Baxter turned from the window. "The very stuff of England," he said quietly.

I smiled. "Those two?"

He nodded.

I was intrigued. "Is there anything particular about them?" I enquired.

"Nothing particular," he said "Just an average good pilot, marrying one of the girls from his station."　　　　　Chapter Nine

Most Secret (1945)

Four very different Allied naval officers aid the French resistance against the Nazis during World War II. Their adventures involve top-secret missions, brutal naval battles, dangerous espionage, and great personal sacrifices.

A NATURAL LEADER

He was quite a merry chap who liked to grease his work with a salacious joke. People liked working for him; he never had any trouble with his staff. In peacetime that was all that one could say about him; it never became apparent till the war was two years old that he was a natural leader of men.   Chapter One

FIRE

"No other weapon purges evil from the earth and rids men from their bondage to the powers of darkness. Only the simple elementals can avail against the elemental foe—faith in the Power of God and in the cleansing power of fire."   Chapter Two

THE ENDURANCE OF TRUTH

There is not one truth in one century, and then another in a later age.   Truth and the Laws of God endure through all the ages of the world.   Chapter Two

OPPRESSED BY A FOREIGN INVADER

"France is a beastly country now.   I never realized just how beastly it all was until I got over here.   Everything - everybody over there …they go round as if they were in a dream, or tied up in a nightmare.   There is a disgusting influence that has sapped their will to work, their will to live.   They move about in lassitude, half men.   They are tools for evil, in the hands of evil men.   And the best of them know it.   And the worst of them enjoy it."   Chapter Two

ISLANDER

Islanders have curious traits in them that break out in the oddest places.

Chapter Three

WAR AND YOUNG PEOPLE

Then the war came.   A war is not a bad time for young people; it brings movement to them, travel, and adventure -- all the things that young people long for.

Chapter Three

OF YORKSHIRE STOCK

The appalling nature of the disaster that might have come to her shook her very much. She came of Yorkshire stock, accustomed to facing facts.

Chapter Three

FAMILY

People without children lived in flats.... but when you had a family you had to do things differently. A family meant you had to have a house ... with lots of children and young people in and out of it. Marriage without kids was a silly business, an affair of flats and cock-tail bars that held no solid Yorkshire happiness. A family meant home and happiness. Chapter Three

DOGS

A lonely man who has a dog grows almost as dependent upon him as does the dog upon his master. Chapter Three

FIGHTING TO WIN

"If you're going to have a fight there's no good sticking to the Marquis of Queensberry's rules."

Chapter Five

AN ARMED INSURGENT

A man with a sub-marine-gun has something tangible to pin his courage to … when things are very bad he can go to it and caress it, and polish it and oil it, and think what he will do with it one day. It gives a purpose to his life. Chapter Ten

Vinland the Good (1945)

The lives and exploits of the
Viking explorers Eric the Red
and his son, Leif Ericson,
retell the Norse sagas of *An
Old Captivity* in this lusty
narrative written in a movie
script format.

THAT KIND OF MAN
"By that time he had been a long time at
sea and he didn't in the least know where he
was, but he went on. He was that kind of
man."   "The Classroom"

HY BREASAIL
"Past the horizon and beyond those rosy
clouds there lies the Happy Land, which this
man called Hy Breasail. No thief, no
robber, and no enemy pursues one there;
there is no violence, and no winter snow. In
that place it is always spring. No flower or
lily is wanting; no rose or violet but you will
find there. There apple trees bear flowers
and fruit on the same branch, all the year
around. There young men live in quiet
happiness with their girls, there is no old age
and no sickness, and no sorrow there. All is
full of joy."   "Leif's Camp"

A GOOD COUNTRY

"A good country is a country where there are good people, a place where men are kind, and generous and simple."

"The River Bank"

HISTORY

"People in history were not a different race from you and me. Your history books deal mostly with the great people, the Kings and Princes and the Ministers of State. They're just the froth upon the surface; the Kings and Princes and the Ministers - they don't mean much. History is made by plain and simple people like ourselves, doing the best we can with each job as it comes along. Leif went out to get timber to build cowhouses, and found America. That's how real people make real history."

"The Classroom"

The Chequer Board (1946)

A shady English businessman discovers he has only a year to live, and devotes his last months to locating and aiding three acquaintances from World War II.

ALL WIVES

He worked on the theory that all foreign wives were exactly and precisely similar to English wives … and if you got someone to translate exactly what you would have said in Watford, it worked out all right.

Chapter Five

ENJOYABLE WORK

All work that interests you is bloody good fun.

Chapter Six

A GOOD MAN

"He is a good man, and will climb up to the Six Blissful Seats. He has known sin and trouble and it has not made him bitter; he has known sorrow and it has not made him sad. In these three months that have been granted to him he is trying to do good, not to avoid damnation, for he has no such beliefs, but for sheer love of good. Such a

man will go up on the Ladder of Existence;
he will not fall back."   Chapter Seven

JUDGE FOR YOURSELF

"You girls are of an age and educated
much the same; you'll hit it off with her all
right if you can just forget what folks have
told you about colour and judge for yourself
from what you see with your own eyes."

Chapter Nine

THE LAW

"Simple people doing the best they can
haven't got much to fear from the law."

Chapter Nine

MARRIAGE

"There's such a sight of things that can go
wrong in a marriage. I don't think colour's
as important as some others—getting on all
right, and respecting one another, and that."

Chapter Ten

BRINGING OUT THE BEST

"I don't think trouble hurts people so
much. I think it kind of brings out what's
the best in them."   Chapter Ten

THE IMPORTANCE OF EDUCATION

"I had been thinking about these darker-
skinned people that I got to know. You

know, there don't seem to be nothing different at all between all of us, only the colour of our skin. I thought somehow they'd be different from that."

His wife said, "You got to remember that those two were different to the general run of dark-skinned people, Jackie. They were educated people."

"That's so," he said thoughtfully. "Maybe there's some sense in paying for all this schooling."   Chapter Eleven

No Highway (1948)

An eccentric aeronautic engineer's quest for truth about transatlantic plane crashes in post-World War II England and Canada involves him in new experiences, controversy, and romance.

THEORETICAL RESEARCH SCIENTISTS

There comes a time when the research worker, disappointed in promotion and secure in his old age if he avoids blotting his copybook, becomes detached from all reality.... As bodily weakness gradually puts an end to physical adventure he turns readily to the adventures of the mind, to the purest realms of thought where in the nature of things no unpleasant consequences can follow if he makes a mistake.

Chapter One

UNDERSTANDING A MAN

After three marriages and thirty years of adult life, she now felt that you never really knew a man until you knew his secret interests.

Chapter Four

A MAN'S INTERESTS

The fact that his interests spread very wide doesn't mean that he's mad. It means that he's sane.   Chapter Six

A Town Like Alice/The Legacy
(1950)

A young typist in post-World War II London uses an unexpected inheritance to pay back a debt to the people in Malaya who saved her life during the war; her generosity results in a new and exciting life in Australia.

TAKING ONE'S TIME WHEN MAKING A DECISION

"I've made plenty of mistakes in my time and I've learned one thing from them, that it's never very wise to do anything in a hurry."   Chapter One

PEOPLE UNDER DISTRESS

Men and women who are in great and prolonged distress and forced into an entirely novel way of life, divorced entirely from their previous associations, frequently develop curious mental traits.

Chapter Four

WORKING IN THE RICE FIELDS

Working in these [rice] fields is not unpleasant when you get accustomed to it.

There are worse things to do in a very hot country than to put on a large conical sun-hat of plaited palm leaves and take off most of your clothes, and play about with mud and water, damming and diverting little trickling streams. Chapter Four

THE NEED TO CREATE A TOWN
LIKE ALICE SPRINGS

"I'm not being very reasonable, am I?" [Jean said.] "First I say I couldn't stand living in a place like that, and then I say that you oughtn't to think of living anywhere else."

"That's right." He was puzzled and distressed. "We've got to try and work it out some way to find out what suits us both."

"There's only one way to do that, Joe."

"What's that?"

She smiled at him. "We'll have to do something about Willstown."

Chapter Seven

FRIENDLY COMPETION, AUSSIE STYLE

"Why can you let each other's poddys [unbranded calves] alone?"

"I'll let his alone, but he won't let mine alone. You see," he said simply, "I got about fifty more of his last year than he got of mine." Chapter Ten

THE BIRTH OF A NEW CITY

It seems to me that I have been mixed up in things far greater than I realized at the time. It is no small matter to assist in the birth of a new city, and as I sit here looking out into the London mists I sometimes wonder just what it is that Jean has done; if any of us realize, even yet, the importance of her achievement. Chapter Eleven

Round the Bend (1951)

After World War II in the Middle and Far East, an airplane mechanic preaches a new gospel based on a positive work ethic, touching many different people throughout the world.

ROMANCE

After six months … we came to the conclusion that we were in love, and we'd get married when the work let up a bit. We didn't realize we both loved something better than each other. I was in love with aeroplanes, and she was in love with love.

Chapter One

FIRST LOVE

You can only do a thing for the first time once, and that goes for falling in love. You may do it over and over again afterwards, but it's never the same. When you chuck away what's given to you that first time, it's chucked away for good.

Chapter Two

YOU CAN BE VERY, VERY CRUEL

You can be very, very cruel just by acting with restraint, and everyone will say what a good chap you are. You can kill somebody just by doing nothing, and be complimented at the inquest. You can be absolutely right all through. And what you'll get from it is a memory of happiness that might have been, if you had acted a little kinder.

Chapter Two

FRIENDSHIP

I was terribly glad to see Connie again. He was a part of my youth, part of the fine time you have before you have to take responsibilities. Presently, as you go through your life, you undertake so many duties that you haven't time for making new, close friendships anymore; you've got too much to do. For the remainder of your life you have to make do with the friends you gathered in your short youth.

Chapter Three

THE PATH OF PEACE

"You yourself must make the effort. Buddhas only show the way. Cut down the love of self as one cuts the lotus in the autumn. Give yourself to following the Path of Peace."

Chapter Three

WORK AS AN EXTENSION OF RELIGION

"We are a peculiar people," he was saying, "we who care for aeroplanes. For common men it is enough to pray five times in each day, as the Imam dictates and as is ordained in the Koran. But we are different, we engineers. We are called to a higher task than common men, and Allah will require much more from us than that."

"With every piece of work you do, with every nut you tighten down, with every filter that you clean or every tappet that you set, pause at each stage and turn to Mecca.... So if the work is good you may proceed in peace."   Chapter Four

MEN'S FOOLISHNESS

"Men are weak, and sinful, and foolish creatures. When they are given something that is beautiful and good they can recognize it and they venerate it, but gradually they spoil it. Infinite wisdom, infinite purity, and infinite holiness cannot be passed from hand to hand by mortal men down through the ages without being spoiled. Errors and absurdities creep in and mar the perfect vision."   Chapter Four

A NEW TEACHER

"Every religion in the world requires to be refreshed from time to time by a new

Teacher. Gautama, Mahomet, Jesus—these are some of the great Teachers of the past, who have refreshed men's minds and by their lives and example brought men back to Truth." Chapter Four

FAR FROM THE TRUTH

"We are far from the Truth now, far enough here, even further in the West. Belsen and Buchenwald exceeded any horrors of the war here in the East. But we are all in this together, wandering, far, far from the Truth." Chapter Four

A SMALL TOWN

A small town's a small town, wherever it is. Chapter Five

TROUBLE

When you're in a bit of trouble I think your mind goes back to childhood, to the time when you had no responsibilities, when all decisions were made for you.

Chapter Six

BUSINESS NO LONGER BEING FUN

I think it was on that day that my business stopped being fun. Up till then, it had been a game to me. I had made money out of it, it is a true, but this had been a paper profit that I had seen nothing of.... It was a game to all of us in those first years, a game that we played together as a team. We had all been of the same mind, I think; the fun that we had in working the thing up together had been the real essence of it. Now, it seemed, the team was to be broken up, and we should go on one man short. Fun is a delicate flower that doesn't stand up very well to changes of that sort. You can't play about with fun.   Chapter Seven

PENANCE

"You gave up England, and wealth, and an easy life in a beautiful place, and love, and the children you long for. You gave up all these things, and came back to the Persian Gulf. Why did you do that...?"

I said, "One does what one thinks is for the best."

"You thought it for the best to give up all the delights of the world, and come back to this hot barren place of difficulties and insults, "he observed. "Why did you do that, you hard-headed man? Did you do it for a penance?"

"I don't know," I said. "If I did, I've got plenty to do penance for."

"So have all men," he replied. "But all men don't do it."   Chapter Seven

RIGHT AND WRONG

"Half a thou too small," he said. "The difference between Right and Wrong. Half a thou bigger, and it'ld be Right. As it is, it's Wrong, and you can't cheat about it."

Chapter Seven

THE POWER OF THE JOB

This power of the job, so much greater than we ourselves! When a good man employs others he becomes a slave to the job, for the job is the guarantee for the security of many men.

Chapter Eight

MONEY AND POWER

"Great money is great power.... And power corrupts. Many evils spring from power.... Even from the power to do good. *All* power corrupts, and the intention to do good has little influence on the corruption."

Chapter Ten

The Far Country (1952)

A young woman from socialist England and an immigrant Czechoslovakian doctor meet and romance in Australia in the early 1950s.

AUSTRALIAN TO THE CORE
He was Australian to the core, bred in the country with only a few years of school in town, an individualist to the bone, a foe of all regimentation and control.

Chapter Six

FAMILY
"When you leave your own place and you start again in a new country, with nobody that you know, it is wonderful to find that someone of your family has been there before."

Chapter Seven

LEADERS
"It is a great thing to have a King, a leader, to prevent the politicians and the bureaucrats from growing stupid. The Germans had the same idea in seeking for a Führer, only they had the wrong man. The English have managed much better. The Americans have also discovered great men for their

Presidents, in some way that is difficult to understand."   Chapter Eight

FLY FISHING

"It [fly fishing] is very delicate, and always one is learning something new. That is why I like it, because never do you come to the end of learning some new thing. Also, it makes you go to beautiful, deserted country."   Chapter Eight

LONELY PEOPLE AND LOVE

Lonely people often think that they're in love, when they aren't really. It must take a long time to be sure you're in love with anybody, and not just lonely.

Chapter Nine

In the Wet (1953)

A parish priest, a dying drunk, and a pilot are the major characters in this futuristic and mystical romantic drama that begins in Australia in the early 1950s and peers thirty years ahead into the political future of the British Commonwealth.

THE AUSTRALIAN MULTIPLE VOTE

"How does your multiple vote work...? What do you get your three votes for?"

"Basic, education, and foreign travel."

"The basic vote—that's what everybody gets, is it?"

"That's right. Everybody gets that at the age of twenty-one."

"And education?"

"That's for higher education. You get it if you take a university degree...."

"And foreign travel?"

"That's for earning your living outside Australia for two years."

"You had a wider outlook than if you'd stayed at home. I suppose that's worth something...." "You can get more votes than three, can't you?"

"You get a vote if you raise two children to the age of fourteen without getting a divorce. You get an extra vote if your personal exertion income … was over five thousand a year…. It's supposed to cater for the man who's got no education and has never been out of Australia and quarreled with his wife, but built up a big business…."

"And the sixth?"

"That's if you're an official of a church…."

"What's the seventh?"

"That's given at the Queen's pleasure. It's more like a decoration…."

"How did it [the multiple vote] come to be taken up?"

"Aw, look….We got a totally different sort of politician when we got the multiple vote. Before that, when it was one man, one vote, the politicians were all tub-thumping nonentities and union bosses. Sensible people didn't stand for parliament. When we got multiple voting we got a better class of politicians altogether, people who got elected by sensible voters…. It was that multiple voting made a nation of Australia."

Chapter Three

RESPONSIBILITY FOR A WEAKENED ENGLAND, CIRCA 1948

"No despot, no autocratic monarch in his pride and greed has injured England so much as the common man. Every penny that could be wrung out of the nation has been devoted to raising the standard of living of the least competent elements in the country, who have held the voting power. No money has been left for generous actions of Great Britain, or for the re-equipment of our industry at home."   Chapter Eight

THE LESSONS OF SCRIPTURE

If the Scriptures teach us anything, it is that God speaks seldom to the wise men or to the great statesmen. For His messages he speaks to poor and humble men, to outcasts, to the people we despise.   Chapter Ten

THE KINGDOM OF HEAVEN

We make our own heaven and our own hell in our own daily lives, and the Kingdom of Heaven is here within us, now.

Chapter Ten

REASONS TO WRITE OF THE FUTURE #1

No man can see into the future, but unless somebody makes a guess from time to time and publishes it to stimulate discussion it seems to me we are drifting in the dark, not knowing where we want to go or how to get there. Author's Note

REASONS TO WRITE OF THE FUTURE #2

Fiction is the most suitable medium in which to ... forecast [the future]. Fiction deals with people and their difficulties and, more than that, nobody takes a novelist too seriously. The puppets born of his imagination walk their little stage for our amusement, and if we find that their creator is impertinent, his errors of taste do not sway the world. Author's Note

Requiem for a Wren/
The Breaking Wave (1955)

A thirty-nine year old Australian, crippled during World War II, arrives home from years of exile in London to discover that a young woman servant at his family's huge cattle station has committed suicide. In unraveling the mystery of her death and life, he discovers much about himself.

THE BEST TIMES

"Until we're dead, we Service people, the world will always be in danger of another war ... For our generation, the war years were the best times of our lives, not because they were war years but because we were young. The best years of our lives happened to be war years. Everyone looks back at the time when they were in their early twenties with nostalgia, but when we look back we only see the war. We had a fine time then, and soon we think we'd have those happy carefree years all over again."

Chapter Seven

TOO PLEASANT

"War's always been too pleasant for the people in it. For most young people it's more attractive as a job than civil service. The vast majority of us never got killed or wounded; we just had a very stimulating and interesting time. If atom bombs can make life thoroughly unpleasant for the people in the Services, in all the countries, then maybe we shall have a chance of peace."

Chapter Seven

MAKING EXCUSES

Whatever I did with my life seemed to be wrong and made unhappiness for everyone concerned. I tried to kid myself it was because I was a cripple, but I knew that wasn't true. You can't evade the consequences of your own actions quite as easily as that. Chapter Seven

Beyond the Black Stump (1956)

> The lives and actions of a young, dedicated American geologist, a feisty Australian woman, and two memorable Irish rogues illustrate the contrasts between the actual and imaginary western frontiers of mid-twentieth century Australia and America.

MOVING DIRT

The urge to move dirt lies deep in the heart of a number of Americans. [Americans love] to use great bulldozers, graders, and Euclids to drive a road through a hill or cut a grade along the shoulder of a mountain.

Chapter One

ABOVE EVERYTHING

"I guess there's one thing above everything a man like me wants in his wife, and that's that she be kind."

Chapter Six

DIFFERENCES BETWEEN A SHEILA
AND A YANK

"We're foreigners … for all that we speak the same language."   Chapter Seven

HONOLULU

As she drifted into sleep that night, the Scot in her began to assert itself; lovely as Honolulu was, and it certainly was by far the loveliest place that she had ever seen, it was in no sense a permanency. It was a place to come to and enjoy and go away from; a place as different to real life as a theatre set.

Chapter Eight

On the Beach (1957)

Several Australians and one American wait in Australia for nuclear death following World War III in this realistic story of the result of the ultimate abuse of science and technology.

RESEARCH

'It's all knowledge. One has to try and find out what has happened. It could be that it's all quite different to what we think … Even if we don't discover anything that's good, it's still discovering things.'

Chapter Two

LOSING THE GAME

"Some games are fun even when you lose. Even when you know you're going to lose before you start. It's fun just finding out."

Chapter Two

OF BRANDY AND BICYCLES

"The last train leaves Flinders Street at eleven-fifteen. I'd better get on that, Dwight. Mummy would never forgive me if I spent the night with you."

"I'll say she wouldn't. What happens when you get to Berwick? Is anyone meeting you?"

She shook her head. "We left a bicycle at the station this morning. If you do the right thing by me I won't be able to ride it, but it's there anyway." She finished her first double brandy. "Buy me another, Dwight."

Chapter Two

DEATH

We've all got to die one day, some sooner and some later. The trouble always has been that you're never ready, because you don't know when it's coming.

Chapter Four

SILLINESS/INSANITY

Some kinds of silliness you just can't stop … if a couple of hundred million people all decide that their national honor requires them to drop cobalt bombs upon their neighbour, well, there's not much that you or I can do about it. The only possible hope would have been to educate them out of their silliness.   Chapter Nine

NEWSPAPERS

We liked our newspapers with pictures of beach girls and headlines about cases of indecent assault, and no government was wise enough to stop us having them that way.   Chapter Nine

The Rainbow and the Rose
(1958)

In the late 1950s, an Australian pilot experiences an eerie out-of-body experience reliving the life of his flying mentor, a veteran flyer of forty years who began his career in England as an RAF pilot during World War I.

A BITTER WOMAN

She was a bitter, spiteful woman but she was so because it was beyond her capacity to understand.   Chapter Three

THE WISE FATHER

At that time and for some years afterward it seemed that Dad had never been so stupid. He could be very dense sometimes. I said to him [my father, the coroner] that the [airplane] accident needed a good deal of sifting and investigation. Before the inquest I had tried to make him understand something about aeroplanes, with the superior knowledge of about five hours solo to my credit....But Dad had been pig-headed and legal that day, and had refused to listen to me. It was years before it gradually occurred to me that possibly Dad hadn't been so stupid after all. But he was dead by that time, and I never had a chance to verify my hunch. Chapter Four

ENGLAND

"England in the spring is like a fairyland. The primroses, and the bluebells in the woods!" Chapter Six

WOMEN OF CHARACTER

None of them [young intelligent airline hostesses/stewardesses who were also nurses] stayed longer than a year; because they were hand-picked for their qualities of character the hospitals drew them back.

Chapter Six

STEALING

"When you get to wanting something that doesn't belong to you so badly that you've just got to have it, and you take it—well, that's stealing. You don't let yourself get into that state of mind with other things— with money or motor cars or gold cigarette cases. And you mustn't do it with love. That's stealing just the same." Chapter Seven

Trustee from the Toolroom
(1960)

A practical, straightforward, and uncomplicated British mechanic travels around the world to fulfill a family responsibility, demonstrating great resourcefulness, courage, and integrity.

MAKING HAPPINESS
He would have made more money in the toolroom progressing up from charge-hand to foreman; he would have made more money as an instructor in a technical college. He would not have made more happiness than he had now attained.

Chapter One

FRIENDS AND WOMEN
Friends and women, he knew, never really mixed. Chapter Nine

A LIFE AND A DEATH
This was the end of something that had begun in a slum street of Renfrew near to Glasgow on the far side of the world, through the joys and tears of childhood, the Tiller Girls, John Dermott and the naval life,

and Janice. Who could have thought that it would all end here, on an uninhabited island in the Pacific Ocean? Chapter Nine

WOMEN

"The more I see of women the less I know," replied the chef du port. "At my age it is better to stick to wine." Chapter Ten

PAYMENT

"A guy has a right to be paid for the job he gets mixed up in, whether he's accustomed to that scale of dough or not." Chapter Ten

CONTENTMENT

If you happen to be in the tram from Southall or from Hanwell at about nine o'clock on a Friday morning, you may see a little man get in at West Ealing, dressed in a shabby raincoat over a blue suit. ...He will spend the evening in the workshop, working on the current model. He has achieved the type of life he desires; he wants no other. He is perfectly, supremely happy.

Chapter Eleven

ACKNOWLEDGEMENTS

Numerous people have helped me with this project. I first wish to thank Nevil Shute Norway's daughter, Heather Mayfield, for her support, her suggestions, and for writing the Foreword. I wish to thank Linda Shaughnessy of A.P. Watt and The Trustees of the Estate of the late Nevil Shute Norway for permitting me to use Nevil Shute quotations in this book. I wish to thank three individuals who made major contributions to the book: Dan Telfair for his wise counsel and permitting me to use his quotation about the Centennial and the photo of the Graham Thorley painting; John Anderson, author of the new definitive biography of Nevil Shute, for kindly sharing his vast knowledge of the man and his works; and Laura Schneider for her vital editing and invaluable advice. I wish to thank the following Shutists who helped me in a variety of ways to complete this book: Steve April, Art Cornell, Fred Erisman, John Henry, Pat and Stephen Holzel, Julienne Marks, John Skillin, and Julian Smith. In addition, I wish to take note of the aid and assistance of Marty Brounstein, Jose and Lorraine Cintron, Gerrianne Delaney, Jen Francis Dwyer, Marlene Falken, Marsha

Feldman, Robert M. Fells, Frank Fredo, Larry Friedlander, Wally Hubert, Jason Housman, J. P. Lesser, Sandy Marco, Ted Michelfelder, Christopher Monroe, Susan O'Banion, James Robert Parish, Vince Poisella, Bob Scola, Robert Stidolph, and Mark Van Ness. Finally, I wish to thank the three ladies in my life for their love and encouragement: Janice Allen, Diana Levy, and Michelle Levy.

ABOUT THE AUTHOR

Born in California, raised on Long Island, and a resident of New Jersey for forty years, Bill Levy is a retired special education teacher who now devotes himself to freelance writing and speaking engagements. He is the author of *John Ford: A Bio-Bibliography* (Greenwood Press). He is also the author of three forthcoming books: *The John Ford Stock Company* (Bear Manor Media), *Fifty Forgotten Gems* (BLS Publishers) and *Using Humor to Combat and Conquer Stress* (BLS Publishers). For further information on the author and this and other projects, visit his website at www.BillLevyShares.com

Made in the USA
Charleston, SC
13 December 2012